Introduction

Birds, Butterflies & Blooms will bring a breath of fresh air to your home and to those whom you choose to gift. Each and every project throughout this book was chosen and designed by Chris Malone, one of today's leading quilt designers. She has a distinct style and a flare for whimsy, not to mention color. Chris has put together this vibrant collection of 14 fun and easy quilt projects just for you. Mix and match the coordinating pieces to complete projects that reflect your own personal taste and needs. You'll find something for every room in the house. The entire collection of projects was created with basic fabrics from Timeless Treasures to ensure that they would be available for purchase for some time to come but don't let this stop you from adding your own touches and colors to these lovely projects.

In *Birds, Butterflies & Blooms* you'll also find detailed instructions for the fusible appliqué technique that is used throughout the book along with designer's tips that are given with every project for ideas about other ways to use the motifs. This is a must-have book for the quilter who is looking for style, options and variety.

Meet the Designer

Chris Malone has been sewing and crafting most of her life. As an accomplished sewist, quilter and designer, she has had hundreds of designs published in sewing and quilting publications and has authored several books of her own.

She is a regular contributor to *Quilter's World* magazine and Annie's quilting and sewing book titles. Chris' whimsical style has been a favorite of many quilters and sewists and is easily recognizable at a glance.

Chris resides in the diverse and beautiful Willamette Valley of Oregon.

Table of Contents

General Instructions

You probably already have most of the supplies needed for these projects. Even so, here are a few tips on materials and tools, general assembly instructions and finishing tips you may find helpful.

Basic Tools & Supplies
- Scissors for paper and fabric
- Rotary cutter and mat (optional)
- Nonslip quilting rulers
- Nonpermanent fabric-marking tools
- Template material
- Sewing machine
- Walking or even-feed foot (optional)
- Hand-sewing needles
- Straight pins and pincushion
- Curved safety pins for basting
- Seam ripper
- Steam/dry iron and ironing surface

Fabric & Thread
For best results, use only good-quality 100 percent cotton fabric and quality thread. Your time is worth it. If you are prewashing, do so with ALL of the fabrics being used. Generally, prewashing is not required in quilting.

Fusible Web With Paper Release
There are a lot of appliquéd projects in this book and all have been made using fusible web with paper release and machine blanket-stitched edges. Always follow manufacturer's directions for fusing times as brands do vary. Of course, if you prefer to hand-appliqué or use other methods of machine appliqué, feel free to do so.

Batting
Almost any low- or mid-loft batting will work for these projects. For items that will be subjected to heat, such as hot pads and coasters, using one or two layers of cotton batting along with needle-punched insulated batting is suggested.

A needle-punched insulated batting reflects heat and cold back to the source. This breathable material has deep fibers that prevent conduction and a reflective metalized film that prevents radiant energy from passing through. **Do not add this batting in anything you will be using in the microwave.**

Fabric Glue
Fabric glue is listed on some of the project materials lists. Usually it is described as an optional item, as you can choose to tack the pieces in place by hand. But sometimes, it is easier and more practical to use glue. When using a fabric glue, apply it carefully and sparingly and follow the manufacturer's directions.

Walking or Even-Feed Foot
A walking or even-feed foot attachment for your sewing machine is a very helpful tool when sewing layers, and it is useful for simple quilting patterns as well. This foot feeds the upper and lower layers of fabric through the machine at the same rate.

Pinking Shears
Since a lot of the projects have curved pieces that are sewn and turned, consider adding a pair of pinking shears to your tool box if you don't already have them. If you cut around curved seams with the pinking shears, you eliminate the need to clip the curves with straight-edge scissors, saving some time and effort. Pinking shears can also be used to control fraying on seam edges.

General Assembly Instructions

Read all instructions carefully before beginning each project.

All seams are ¼" unless otherwise directed.

The measurements given for each project include the outer seam allowance.

Press each seam as you sew.

Appliqué

Many of the projects in this book are made using a fusible web with paper release and a machine blanket stitch. Refer to Raw-Edge Fusible Appliqué on page 6 for specifics. Other appliqué methods may be substituted if desired. All of the appliqué patterns are reversed so they will face the correct direction when fused to the background. When appliqués overlap, slip one edge under the other ¼" before fusing.

Sometimes, appliqué fabric is so light colored or thin that the background fabric shows through excessively. You can correct this transparency problem by fusing a piece of lightweight interfacing to the wrong side of the fabric. Then apply the fusible web with the marked pattern to the interfacing side. Cut out and use in the same way.

To add dimension to appliqué pieces, padded appliqué is a method where batting is sewn into the appliqué shape. Refer to Padded Appliqué below for specifics on using this method.

Padded Appliqué

Some of the projects are finished with a "padded" appliqué. In this technique, an appliqué piece is sewn with two layers of fabric and a layer of batting and then turned right side out through an opening. Padded appliqué gives dimensional interest to a project.

1. Prepare template using pattern provided and trace the shape on the wrong side of the selected fabric. Fold the fabric in half with the right sides facing and the traced shape on top.

2. Pin this fabric to a scrap of batting that is slightly larger than traced shape and then sew on the traced lines as shown in Figure A.

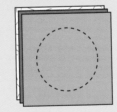

Figure A

3. The instructions will tell you whether you should leave a side opening for turning in the seam allowance, or if you should sew all around and then make a slash in one layer of fabric only for turning.

4. Cut out the shape ⅛"–¼" from the seam line, clip curves generously (or use pinking shears to cut out).

5. To make a slash, pinch the top layer of fabric and pull away that layer from the other fabric layer; make a little snip in the pinched fabric. Insert scissor tips into the hole and cut the fabric just enough to turn the shape right side out (Figure B). If desired, add a little no-fray solution to the cut edges of the slash and let it dry.

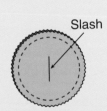

Slash

Figure B

6. After turning the shape right side out through the slash or side opening, whipstitch the cut edges of slash back together as shown in Figure C or slip-stitch the side opening closed. Press the shape from the top side so it is flat and smooth at the edges.

Figure C

Finishing Your Quilts

Prepare batting and backings larger than the quilt top. For bed-size quilts, we suggest battings and backings that are 8" larger than the quilt. For smaller projects, refer to materials lists for sizes.

Quilting

1. Press quilt top on both sides and trim all loose threads.

2. On a flat surface, make a quilt sandwich by layering the backing right side down, the batting on top of the backing and then the quilt top centered right side up on the batting. Make sure each layer is smoothed out. Pin or baste layers together to hold.

3. Use nonpermanent marking tool to mark quilting design on quilt top. Quilt as desired by hand or machine. **Note:** *If you are sending a bed-size quilt to a professional quilter, contact quilter for specifics about preparing your quilt for quilting.*

4. When quilting is complete, remove pins or basting. Trim batting and backing edges even with raw edges of quilt top.

Binding

1. Join binding strips on short ends with diagonal seams to make one long strip; trim seams to ¼" and press seams open (Figure 1).

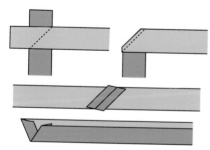

Figure 1

2. Fold 1" of one short end to wrong side and press. Fold the binding strip in half with wrong sides together along length, again referring to Figure 1; press.

3. Starting about 3" from the folded short end of the binding, sew binding to quilt-top edges, matching raw edges and using a ¼" seam. Stop stitching ¼" from corner and backstitch (Figure 2).

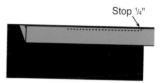

Stop ¼"

Figure 2

4. Fold binding up at a 45-degree angle to seam and then down even with quilt-top edge, forming a pleat at the corner, referring to Figure 3.

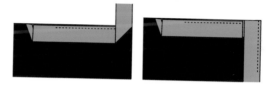

Figure 3

5. Resume stitching from corner edge as shown in Figure 3, down quilt side, backstitching ¼" from next corner. Repeat, mitering all corners, stitching to within 3" of starting point.

6. Trim binding end long enough to tuck inside starting end and compete stitching (Figure 4).

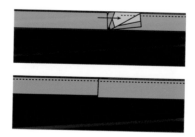

Figure 4

7. Fold binding to quilt back and stitch in place by hand or machine to complete your quilt. ●

Raw-Edge Fusible Appliqué

One of the easiest ways to appliqué is the raw-edge fusible-web method. Paper-backed fusible web individual pieces are fused to the wrong side of specified fabrics, cut out and then fused together in a motif or individually to a foundation fabric, where they are machine-stitched in place.

Choosing Appliqué Fabrics

Depending on the appliqué, you may want to consider using batiks. Batik is a much tighter weave and, because of the manufacturing process, does not fray. If you are thinking about using regular quilting cottons, be sure to stitch your raw-edge appliqués with blanket/buttonhole stitches instead of a straight stitch.

Cutting Appliqué Pieces

1. Fusible appliqué shapes should be reversed for this technique.

2. Trace the appliqué shapes onto the paper side of paper-backed fusible web. Leave at least ¼" between shapes. Cut out shapes leaving a margin around traced lines. **Note:** *If doing several identical appliqués, trace reversed shapes onto template material to make reusable templates for tracing shapes onto the fusible web.*

3. Follow manufacturer's instructions and fuse shapes to wrong side of fabric as indicated on pattern for color and number to cut.

4. Cut out appliqué shapes on traced lines. Remove paper backing from shapes.

5. Again following fusible web manufacturer's instructions, arrange and fuse pieces to quilt referring to quilt pattern. Or fuse together shapes on top of an appliqué ironing mat to make an appliqué motif that can then be fused to the quilt.

Stitching Appliqué Edges

Machine-stitch appliqué edges to secure the appliqués in place and help finish the raw edges with matching or invisible thread (Photo 1). **Note:** *To show stitching, all samples have been stitched with contrasting thread.*

Straight stitch

Buttonhole or blanket stitch

Photo 1

Invisible thread can be used to stitch appliqués down when using the blanket or straight stitches. Do not use it for the satin stitch. Definitely practice with invisible thread before using it on your quilt; it can sometimes be difficult to work with.

A short, narrow buttonhole or blanket stitch is most commonly used (Photo 2). Your machine manual may also refer to this as an appliqué stitch. Be sure to stitch next to the appliqué edge with the stitch catching the appliqué.

Photo 2

Practice turning inside and outside corners on scrap fabric before stitching appliqué pieces. Learn how your machine stitches so that you can make the pivot points smooth.

1. To stitch outer corners, stitch to the edge of the corner and stop with needle in the fabric at the corner point. Pivot to the next side of the corner and continue to sew (Photo 3). You will get a box on an outside corner.

Photo 3

2. To stitch inner corners, pivot at the inner point with needle in fabric (Photo 4). You will see a Y shape in the corner.

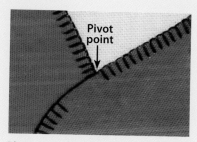

Pivot point

Photo 4

3. You can also use a machine straight stitch. Turn corners in the same manner, stitching to the corners and pivoting with needle in down position (Photo 5).

Photo 5

General Appliqué Tips

1. Use a light- to medium-weight stabilizer behind an appliqué to keep the fabric from puckering during machine stitching (Photo 6).

Photo 6

2. To reduce the stiffness of a finished appliqué, cut out the center of the fusible web shape, leaving ¼"–½" inside the pattern line. This gives a border of adhesive to fuse to the background and leaves the center soft and easy to quilt.

3. If an appliqué fabric is so light colored or thin that the background fabric shows through, fuse a lightweight interfacing to the wrong side of the fabric. You can also fuse a piece of the appliqué fabric to a matching piece, wrong sides together, and then apply the fusible with a drawn pattern to one side.

Mornin' Sunshine Place Mats

These place mats are designed to wake you up
and start your day with a big smile!

Skill Level
Confident Beginner

Specifications
Place Mat Size: 16" x 12"

Materials
Materials listed make 2 place mats.
- Scraps light and medium yellow tonals, light and medium orange tonals and black solid
- ¼ yard black with white dot
- ½ yard aqua dot
- ½ yard aqua tonal
- 2 (14" x 18") cotton batting rectangles
- 2 (14" x 18") insulated batting rectangles
- Template material
- Fusible web with paper release
- Basic sewing tools and supplies

Project Notes
Read all instructions before beginning this project.

Stitch right sides together using a ¼" seam allowance unless otherwise specified.

Refer to General Instructions on page 3 for specific construction and appliqué tips and techniques.

Materials and cutting lists assume 40" of usable fabric width.

Cutting

From black with white dot:
- Cut 3 (2¼" by fabric width) binding strips.

From aqua dot:
- Cut 2 (12½" x 16½") A rectangles.

From aqua tonal:
- Cut 2 (12½" x 16½") backing rectangles

Assembling the Place Mats
Refer to the Placement Diagram and project photo throughout for positioning of pieces and stitching lines.

1. Prepare appliqué templates using patterns listed and provided on the insert for these place mats: Letters: m, o, r, n, i, ' (apostrophe), s, u, h and e; Quarter Sun; Place Mat Sun Ray; and Butterfly Motif.

2. Trace appliqué shapes onto paper side of fusible web referring to list below for number to trace; cut out. Apply shapes to wrong side of fabrics as listed below.

- Light yellow tonal: 2 quarter suns
- Medium yellow tonal: 6 place mat sun rays and 2 butterfly large spots
- Light orange tonal: 4 place mat sun rays and 2 butterfly small spots
- Medium orange tonal: 2 each letters: m, o, r, '(apostrophe), u, h, and e; 4 each letters: i and s; 8 letters: n; and 2 butterfly wings
- Black solid: 2 butterfly bodies

Here's a Tip

If you don't want to make a set of place mats, you can use this pattern to make a cute wall hanging. Make it the same as for the place mat but add a border to enlarge it a bit.

3. Cut out and arrange appliqué shapes on A rectangles; fuse in place.

4. Machine blanket-stitch around each appliqué shape using matching thread.

5. Layer a backing rectangle, right side down; an insulated batting rectangle, shiny side down; a cotton batting rectangle and a place mat top right side up and centered. Repeat for second place mat. Baste and quilt as desired. Model is stitched around all the appliqué shapes with matching thread. The sun and rays are outline-quilted ¼" inside the outer edges.

6. Machine double-stitch butterfly antennae with black thread.

7. Trim backing and batting to the same size as top if necessary.

8. Bind edges with the binding strip referring to General Instructions on page 3. ●

Mornin' Sunshine Place Mat
Placement Diagram 16" x 12"

Sunshine & Flowers Wall Hanging

The warm sunshine helps the beautiful flowers bloom, and that's what this wall hanging celebrates.

Skill Level
Confident Beginner

Specifications
Wall Hanging Size: 9" x 38"
Block Size: 9" x 9" finished
Number of Blocks: 3

Materials
- Scraps light and medium yellow tonals
- Fat eighth aqua dot
- ⅛ yard yellow dot
- ½ yard white tonal
- ⅝ yard lime dot
- 1 each 9½" x 32½" and 7" x 10" batting rectangles
- Thread
- Fusible web with paper release
- Template material
- 2 (1") plastic rings
- Basic sewing tools and supplies

Project Notes
Read all instructions before beginning this project.

Stitch right sides together using a ¼" seam allowance unless otherwise specified.

Refer to General Instructions on page 3 for specific construction and appliqué tips and techniques.

Materials and cutting lists assume 40" of usable fabric width.

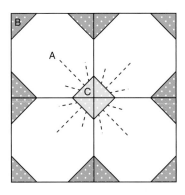

Flower
9" x 9" Finished Block
Make 3

Cutting

From aqua dot:
- Cut 1 (6" x 9½") D rectangle.

From yellow dot:
- Cut 1 (1¾" by fabric width) strip.
    Subcut strip into 12 (1¾") C squares.

From white tonal:
- Cut 2 (5" by fabric width) strips.
    Subcut strips into 12 (5") A squares.

From lime dot:
- Cut 2 (2" by fabric width) strips.
    Subcut strips into 36 (2") B squares.
- Cut 1 (9½" x 32½") backing rectangle.

Assembling the Wall Hanging
Refer to the Placement Diagram and project photo throughout for positioning of pieces.

1. Prepare templates using patterns listed and provided on the insert for the wall hanging: Small Half Sun, Small Sun Ray and Leaf 3.

2. Trace the Small Half Sun and Small Sun Ray appliqué shapes onto paper side of fusible web referring to list below for number to trace; cut out shapes. Apply shapes to wrong side of fabrics as listed below.

- Light yellow tonal: 1 small half sun
- Medium yellow tonal: 7 small sun rays

3. Cut out and arrange appliqué shapes on D rectangle, centering the half sun on one 9½" edge of the rectangle; fuse shapes in place.

4. Machine blanket-stitch around each appliqué shape using matching thread.

5. Draw a diagonal line on the wrong side of each B and C square.

6. Place a C square on one corner and B squares on remaining corners of an A square referring to Figure 1.

Figure 1

7. Stitch on the drawn lines and trim seams to ¼" (Figure 2). Flip triangles and press.

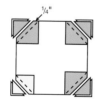

Figure 2

8. Repeat steps 6 and 7 to make 12 units.

9. Referring to the block drawing, arrange four units so yellow triangles are in the center. Sew units into rows; press. Sew rows together to complete the Flower block; press. Repeat to make a total of three Flower blocks.

10. Arrange and sew D and the three flower blocks in a vertical row; press.

11. Referring to the Padded Appliqué instructions on page 4, make two leaves using the prepared Leaf 3 template, 7" x 10" batting rectangle and remaining lime dot fabric. Referring to Leaf 3 pattern for placement, quilt vein lines in each leaf using green thread.

12. Pin and baste the leaves to the bottom Flower block of the wall hanging, right sides together with the raw edges matching and a ¾" space between the two leaves.

13. Using the cutting pattern provided on the insert, mark rounded shape and trim the top edge of the wall hanging top (D) and one end of the backing rectangle.

14. Layer batting, backing rectangle right side up and wall hanging top right side down. Stitch around edge through all layers, leaving a 5" opening on one side. Trim batting close to the seam; trim corners and clip curves; turn right side out. Fold in seam allowance on the opening and slip-stitch closed. Press the edges smooth and flat.

15. Quilt as desired. Model is stitched in the ditch around yellow centers of block and stitched ¼" from the seam around the flowers. Three lines are stitched in each petal. Stitching outlines the sun and ray appliqué shapes. The Flower blocks are topstitched ¼" from outer seam.

16. Sew plastic rings near top on the back for hanging. ●

Here's a Tip

Use the Flower block as the basis for a quilt by making multiple Flower blocks to sew together to the desired size. The flower blocks can be all the same color or scrappy with lots of color. Sashing can be added between the blocks to separate them. A pretty border fabric will increase the size of the quilt and make a nice finish.

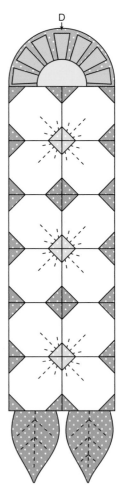

Sunshine & Flowers Wall Hanging
Placement Diagram 9" x 38"

Welcome Wreath

What better way to say "Welcome" than with this beautiful wreath hanging on your door or hanging in your entry hall.

Skill Level

Confident Beginner

Specifications

Wreath Size: 14" x 14"

Materials

- Scraps orange, pink, aqua and yellow tonals, and aqua dot
- Fat quarter each white tonal and lime tonal
- ½ yard yellow dot
- Cotton batting
- 14" foam wreath
- Fiberfill
- Thread
- 2 (1⅛") cover button kits
- 1 (¾") cover button kit
- 2 (³⁄₁₆") black buttons
- 8" length 22-gauge black wire
- 1 (½") plastic ring
- Fabric glue
- Basic sewing tools and supplies

Project Notes

Read all instructions before beginning this project.

Stitch right sides together using a ¼" seam allowance unless otherwise specified.

Refer to General Instructions on page 3 for specific construction tips and techniques.

Materials and cutting lists assume 40" of usable fabric width.

Cutting

From yellow dot:

- Cut 4 (3½" by fabric width) strips.

From cotton batting:

- Cut 3" strips to total 160" in length.

Completing the Embellishments

Refer to the Padded Appliqué instructions on page 4 to make embellishments.

1. Trace the embellishment pieces listed below on the wrong side of the fabrics.

- White tonal: 7 small daisy petals and 14 large daisy petals
- Pink tonal: 9 tulip petals 1
- Lime tonal: 6 small leaves (reverse 3) and 6 large leaves (reverse 3)
- Aqua tonal: 1 bird body 2
- Aqua dot: 2 bird wings 3
- Orange tonal: 1 bird beak 2 and 1 butterfly 2

2. Fold each marked fabric in half, right sides together, and pin to scraps of batting. Do not pin the bird body to the batting at this time.

3. Sew around each small and large petal on traced lines, leaving each petal open at the bottom straight edge. Trim the batting and cut out each piece ⅛" from the seam. Turn right side out and press edges smooth and flat. Topstitch ¼" from the edges of each petal and up through the center, about ⅔ of the way (Figure 1).

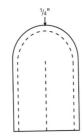

¼"

Figure 1

4. Using matching doubled thread, hand-sew several gathering stitches across the bottom of one small petal. Pick up a second small petal and stitch across the bottom with the same thread and pull to gather as shown in Figure 2.

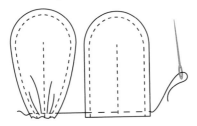

Figure 2

5. Continue to stitch and gather until all seven small petals are attached. Make a stitch back into the first petal to gather the petals into a tight circle as shown in Figure 3. Knot and clip thread.

Figure 3

6. Repeat steps 4 and 5 with the large daisy petals to make two large daisies.

7. Cover three cover buttons with yellow tonal fabric following manufacturer's directions.

8. Glue the ¾" covered button to the center of the small daisy and a 1⅛" button to the center of each large daisy.

9. Sew all around each tulip petal on traced lines. Cut out each petal ⅛" from the seam. Make a slash through one layer of fabric only. Turn each petal right side out through the slash and press the edges smooth and flat. Whipstitch slash edges closed. Topstitch around each petal ¼" from the edge.

10. Arrange petals in groups of three each with one in the center and the other two overlapping on each side (Figure 4). Use a few dots of glue to secure the petals.

Figure 4

11. Sew all around leaves on traced lines. Cut out each leaf ⅛" from the seam. Make a slash through one layer of fabric only. Turn each leaf right side out through the slash and press the edges smooth and flat. Whipstitch slash edges together.

12. Stitch vein lines as desired on each completed leaf using a darker green thread.

13. Sew all around butterfly on traced lines. Cut out ⅛" from the seam. Make a slash through one layer of fabric only. Turn the butterfly right side out through the slash and press the edges smooth and flat. Whipstitch the slash edges closed. Topstitch around ⅛" from the edge. Stitch down the center of the butterfly and, if desired, stitch oval shapes in the wings as shown on Placement Diagram.

14. To make the butterfly antennae, fold the wire in half and then shape each end into tight concentric circles. Stitch the center fold to the top center of the butterfly (Figure 5) and then sew a small black button over the stitches for butterfly's head.

Figure 5

15. To finish the bird, sew on traced lines of the beak, leaving open at the straight edge opposite the rounded point. Cut out ⅛" from the seam; turn right side out.

16. To make it easier to position the beak, cut out the bird body front and back about ¼" from the traced line. This does not have to be exact since you have already drawn the sewing line. Referring to the pattern for positioning, place the beak inside the bird head, between the front and back, which are right sides together. The open end of the beak should be at the edge of the cut fabric as shown in Figure 6. Baste or pin to secure and then pin the bird body to a scrap of batting.

Figure 6

17. Sew all around on traced line, leaving open where indicated on the pattern. Trim the batting and clip the curves. At the neck seam, snip close to, but not through, the seam line. Turn right side out. Stuff very lightly with a small amount of fiberfill and fold in the edges of the seam allowance on the opening. Slip-stitch the folded edges together to close.

18. Sew around wings on traced lines. Cut out ⅛" from the seam. Make a slash through one layer of fabric only. Turn the wings right side out through the slashes and press the edges smooth and flat. Whipstitch slash edges closed.

19. Referring to Figure 7, position the wings on the bird, one in front and one behind the body as shown, with the slashed sides down. Tack the wings in place by stitching the wide end of the wing to the bird and leaving the pointed end free.

Figure 7

20. Sew the black button to the bird for an eye.

Assembling the Wreath

1. Join the 3½" yellow dot strips on the short ends to make one long strip. Fold and press a ½" hem on one long edge of the strip.

2. Butt short ends of batting strips and join to make a long strip.

3. Place the batting strip on the wrong side of the yellow dot strip with one long edge tucked under the folded hem (Figure 8). Pin to secure, placing the pins on the outside of the fabric for easy removal later.

Figure 8

4. Pin one end of the fabric/batting strip at the back of the wreath and begin to spiral-wrap the strip around the wreath, overlapping the edges and keeping it snug against the wreath form (Figure 9). When the wreath is completely covered, trim the end as necessary and glue or whipstitch it to the back of the wreath.

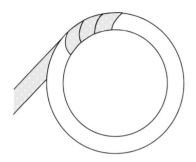

Figure 9

5. Referring to the Placement Diagram and project photo, arrange the leaves, tulips and daisies across the bottom of the wreath, letting the arrangement flow up the sides as shown. Use pins to hold the pieces in place. Tuck the bird in place behind a leaf on the right side and place the butterfly on the upper left side of wreath.

6. When satisfied with the arrangement, lift each piece one at a time, starting with the pieces in the back, and apply glue carefully before replacing it. Try to keep the pieces dimensional by just gluing the centers of the flowers and the base of the leaves. Apply glue in a line on the center back of the butterfly so the wings remain free. ***Note:*** *If desired, you can use small pins strategically to attach all the*

components instead of using glue. This way, you can remove them when you need to store the wreath or even reuse the wreath for other seasonal decorations.

7. Sew the plastic ring to the top back of the wreath for a hanger. ●

Here's a Tip

Any of these dimensional quilted pieces can be used to decorate other surfaces. Use them on a basket, a picture frame or attach a pin back to use on clothing.

Welcome Wreath
Placement Diagram 14" x 14"

Early Bird Mug Rugs

The early bird does indeed get the worm, and she loves to sing about it. This set of mug rugs is quick and easy to make, and practical too.

Skill Level
Confident Beginner

Specifications
Mug Rug Size: 8½" x 6½"

Materials
Materials listed make 2 mug rugs.
- Scraps each yellow dot, pink dot, light yellow tonal, light pink tonal and brown solid
- Fat quarter light blue tonal
- ⅓ yard lime dot
- 2 (6½" x 8½") rectangles cotton batting
- 2 (6½" x 8½") rectangles insulated batting
- Black embroidery floss
- 2 (³⁄₁₆") black buttons
- 2 (¼") black buttons
- Fusible web with paper release
- Basic sewing tools and supplies

Project Notes
Read all instructions before beginning this project.

Stitch right sides together using a ¼" seam allowance unless otherwise specified.

Refer to General Instructions on page 3 for specific construction and appliqué tips and techniques.

Materials and cutting lists assume 40" of usable fabric width.

Cutting

From light blue tonal:
- Cut 1 (6½" x 8½") A rectangle, 1 (5¼" x 8½") B rectangle and 2 (6½" x 8½") backing rectangles.

From lime dot:
- Cut 1 (1¾" by fabric width) strip. Subcut strip into 1 (1¾" x 8½") C strip.
- Cut 2 (2¼" by fabric width) binding strips.

Completing the Mug Rugs
Refer to the Placement Diagram and project photo throughout for positioning of pieces.

1. Sew the C strip to one long edge of a B rectangle to make B-C unit; press.

2. Prepare appliqué templates using patterns listed and provided on the insert for these mug rugs: Leaf 2, Worm, Branch, Bird Wing 1 and 2, Bird Body 1, Tail Feathers, Beak 1 and Singing Bird Beak and Musical Notes.

3. Trace appliqué shapes onto paper side of fusible web referring to list below for number to trace; cut out. Apply shapes to wrong side of fabrics as listed below.

- Yellow dot: 1 each wing 1, wing 2 and tail feathers (each reversed); 1 each beak 1 and singing bird beak
- Pink dot: 1 each wing 1, wing 2 and tail feathers
- Light yellow tonal: 1 bird body 1 (reversed)
- Light pink tonal: 1 bird body 1
- Brown solid: 1 each worm and branch
- Lime dot: 3 leaf 2

4. Cut out appliqué shapes. Refer to Figure 1 to place branch on A and to Figure 2 to place bird body 1 on B. Arrange remaining shapes on A and B-C unit; fuse in place.

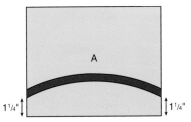

Figure 1

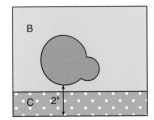

Figure 2

5. Machine blanket-stitch around each appliqué shape using matching thread.

6. Layer the backing, right side down; insulated batting, shiny side up; cotton batting rectangle and the mug rug top right side up and centered. Baste and quilt as desired. Models are stitched around all the appliqué shapes.

7. Using black thread, machine double-stitch pink bird's legs on B-C unit and musical notes on A. Stitch French knot using two strands of black embroidery floss for the worm's eye.

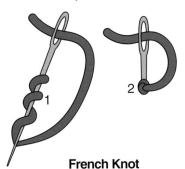

French Knot

8. Referring to the photo and the insert, sew the ³⁄₁₆" buttons to each bird for eyes and the ¼" buttons to the bottom of musical note stitching.

9. Trim backing and batting to the same size as top if necessary.

10. Bind edges with the binding strip referring to General Instructions on page 3. ●

Here's a Tip

Mug rugs make wonderful gifts, especially if you include a mug and coordinate the fabric to match it. Put the mugs rugs and mugs in a basket with coffee, tea or hot chocolate packets, along with biscotti or cookies, and it becomes a very special treat.

Early Bird Mug Rugs
Placement Diagrams 8¹⁄₂" x 6¹⁄₂"

Branching Out Hot Pads

It's always nice to have a few hot pads to protect the table, and it's even better when they coordinate with the table runner! These are very quick to make with big, bold appliqués and no binding.

Skill Level
Confident Beginner

Specifications
Hot Pad Size: 9" x 9"

Materials
Materials listed make one each style of hot pad.
- Scraps red, pink, orange, yellow, green and light orange tonals, and black solid
- ⅓ yard white with black dot
- ⅜ yard black with white dot
- 2 (9½") squares cotton batting
- 2 (9½") squares insulated batting
- Thread
- Template material
- Fusible web with paper release
- Basic sewing tools and supplies

Project Notes
Read all instructions before beginning this project.

Stitch right sides together using a ¼" seam allowance unless otherwise specified.

Refer to General Instructions on page 3 for specific construction and appliqué tips and techniques.

Materials and cutting lists assume 40" of usable fabric width.

Cutting

From white with black dot:
- Cut 2 (7") A squares.

From black with white dot:
- Cut 1 (9½" by fabric width) strip.
  Subcut strip into 2 (9½") backing squares, 4 (1¾" x 9½") C strips and 4 (1¾" x 7") B strips.

Assembling the Hot Pads

Refer to the Placement Diagram and project photo throughout for positioning of pieces.

1. Prepare appliqué templates using patterns listed and provided on the insert for this table runner: Butterfly Motif, Small Flower, Small Flower Center and Stem; and Large Flower and Large Flower Center.

2. Trace appliqué shapes onto paper side of fusible web referring to list below for number to trace; cut out. Apply shapes to wrong side of fabrics as listed below.

- Red tonal: 1 large flower
- Yellow tonal: 1 each large and small flower center, 1 large butterfly spot
- Pink tonal: 1 small flower
- Green tonal: 1 stem
- Orange tonal: butterfly wing
- Black solid: butterfly body
- Light orange tonal: small butterfly spot

3. Cut out and arrange appliqué shapes on A squares; fuse in place.

4. Machine blanket-stitch around each appliqué shape using matching thread.

5. To complete each hot pad top, sew B strips to opposite sides and C strips to top and bottom of each A square, pressing after each seam.

6. Position a backing square with a hot pad top, right sides facing, and layer on top of one each cotton batting square and insulated batting square, shiny side down; pin layers to secure. Sew around edges leaving a 4-inch opening in one side. Trim corners and turn right side out. Fold in seam allowance and slip-stitch closed. Press edges flat and smooth.

7. Repeat step 6 with remaining top, backing and batting squares.

8. Quilt as desired. Model is stitched around each appliqué shape using matching thread. Stitch in the ditch between the border and center and topstitch ¼" from edge. Butterfly antennae is double-stitched with black thread. ●

Here's a Tip

Reduce the size of the patterns and use them to make coasters—always a welcome gift!

Branching Out Hot Pads
Placement Diagrams 9" x 9"

Flower Bench Pillow

The big and bold blooms on this pillow give it loads of personality and pizzazz. The dimensional flowers are made with circular petals that are surprisingly easy to make.

Skill Level
Confident Beginner

Specifications
Pillow Size: 28" x 14"

Materials
- Scraps yellow tonal and light orange tonal
- ⅓ yard white tonal
- ⅜ yard pink tonal
- ⅜ yard pink dot
- ½ yard lime dot
- ¾ yard lime tonal
- Cotton batting
- 28" x 14" pillow form
- 1 yard lightweight interfacing
- ¼ yard heavyweight interfacing
- 4 (1½") cover button kits
- 4" black 1mm round shoelace or 8" length of 22-gauge black wire
- 1 (³⁄₁₆") black button
- Template material
- Fabric glue
- Basic sewing tools and supplies

Project Notes
Read all instructions before beginning this project.

Stitch right sides together using a ¼" seam allowance unless otherwise specified.

Refer to General Instructions on page 3 for specific construction tips and techniques.

Materials and cutting lists assume 40" of usable fabric width.

Cutting

From white tonal:
- Cut 2 (4" by fabric width) strips.
  Subcut strips into 16 (4") A squares.

From pink tonal:
- Cut 3 (3¼" by fabric width) strips.
  Subcut strips into 32 (3¼") B squares.

From pink dot:
- Cut 3 (3¼" by fabric width) strips.
  Subcut strips into 32 (3¼") B squares.

From lime tonal:
- Cut 2 (4" by fabric width) strips.
  Subcut strips into 16 (4") A squares.
- Cut 1 (14½" by fabric width) strip.
  Subcut strip into 2 (14½" x 16½") backing rectangles.

From batting:
- Cut 1 (28½" x 14½") rectangle and 1 (12" x 18") rectangle.

From lightweight interfacing:
- Cut 32 (3¼") squares.

From heavyweight interfacing:
- Cut 4 (2") circles.

Assembling the Pillow
Refer to the Placement Diagram and project photo throughout for positioning of pieces.

1. Arrange lime and white A squares into four rows of eight squares each, alternating colors. Sew the squares together in each row. Sew the rows together to make the pillow front.

2. Pin or baste the pillow front to the 28½" x 14½" batting rectangle. Quilt as desired. Model is stitched ¼" from the seams and diagonally through all the white squares.

3. Prepare templates using patterns listed and provided on the insert for this pillow: Round Petal, Leaf 7 and Butterfly 2.

4. Trace the round petal shape on the wrong side in the center of each pink tonal B square. Stack a lightweight interfacing square, a pink dot B square, right side up, and a pink tonal B square right side down; pin layers together. Sew on traced line, leaving a 1" opening (Figure 1). Cut around circle ⅛" from the seam using pinking shears. Turn the petal right side out. Do not close the opening.

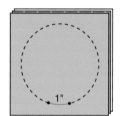

Figure 1

5. Press the petal flat from the pink dot side. With the opening at the bottom and referring to Figure 2, fold in two sides at an angle to make pink tonal "wings." Stitch across the bottom ⅜" from the edge to secure. Repeat to make 32 petals.

Make 32

—⅜"

Figure 2

6. Referring to Figure 3, arrange eight petals on each heavy-weight interfacing circle. Petals should extend about 2" over the edge of the interfacing and leave a small opening in the center. The sides of each petal should touch but not overlap each other.

Remove one petal at a time and apply a few dots of glue to the back. Return it to its position and repeat with all petals in each circle to make four flowers.

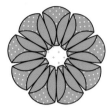

Figure 3

7. Referring to Padded Appliqué instructions on page 4, make seven lime dot fabric leaves and one light orange tonal butterfly.

8. Refer to Leaf 7 pattern to quilt each leaf by stitching a vein pattern using green thread.

9. Referring to Figure 4, topstitch butterfly about ⅛" from the seam. Stitch down the center of the butterfly and, if desired, stitch oval shapes in the wings.

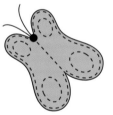

Figure 4

10. Arrange flowers across the pillow front and tuck the leaves under the petals. Add the butterfly between the three flowers on the right. When satisfied with the arrangement, pin the leaves and butterfly in place and remove the flowers. Sew the leaves to the pillow front by stitching over the center vein line using the same green thread. Sew the butterfly in place by stitching down the center with the same orange thread.

11. To make the butterfly antennae, fold the shoelace in half and tack the folded end in place at the top of the butterfly, again referring to Figure 4. Using the same thread, sew the black button over the tacking stitches. ***Note:*** *If you prefer, follow the directions in step 14 of the Welcome Wreath on page 16 to use wire for the antennae.*

12. To prepare the pillow backs, press and sew a double ¼" hem on one short edge of each piece.

13. Referring to Figure 5, with right sides together, pin a pillow back to each end of the pillow front, matching raw edges and with the hemmed ends overlapping in the center. Sew around the pillow with a ¼" seam allowance. Trim the corners and turn right side out.

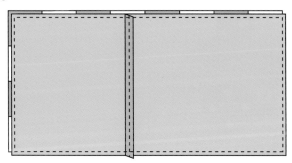

Figure 5

14. Cover the buttons with yellow tonal following manufacturer's directions. Sew the shank of each button to the center of a flower through the interfacing.

15. Reposition the flowers on the pillow front and attach by sewing the edge of the interfacing to the pillow by hand.

16. Insert pillow form into the pillow to complete. ●

Here's a Tip

These flowers are such a fun embellishment they could be used on many things including totes, baskets and even quilts. Another use for the petals is to line them up in a row, instead of around a circle, and use them for a border.

Flower Bench Pillow
Placement Diagram 28" x 14"

Here's a Tip

These two appliqué designs could be used on many other items around the house, such as pillowcases, a quilted tea cozy or an apron bib.

Busy Garden Tea Towels

Just a bit of appliqué, a few buttons and a strip of dotted fabric can add that special touch to a purchased tea towel.

Skill Level
Confident Beginner

Specifications
Tea Towel Size: 20" x 28"

Materials
- Scraps white, yellow and red tonals; black with white dot; white with black crosshatch; lime dot and black solid
- ⅛ yard each yellow dot and white with black dot
- Thread
- 1 each purchased lime green and chambray tea towels
- 3 (¾") green flower-shape buttons
- 2 (¾") black-and-white buttons
- 1 (³⁄₁₆") black button
- Template material
- Black and white embroidery floss
- Fusible web with paper release
- Fusible interfacing
- Basic sewing tools and supplies

Project Notes
Read all instructions before beginning this project.

Stitch right sides together using a ¼" seam allowance unless otherwise specified.

Refer to General Instructions on page 3 for specific construction and appliqué tips and techniques.

Materials and cutting lists assume 40" of usable fabric width.

Cutting

From yellow dot:
- Cut 1 (2¾" by fabric width) strip.
  Subcut strip into 1 (2¾" by width of tea towel plus 1") strip for band.

From white with black dot:
- Cut 1 (2¾" by fabric width) strip.
  Subcut strip into 1 (2¾" by width of tea towel plus 1") strip for band.

From fusible interfacing:
- Cut 2 (1¾" by width of tea towel) strips.

Completing the Tea Towels
Refer to the Placement Diagrams and project photo throughout for positioning of pieces and stitching.

1. Prewash, dry and press tea towels.

2. Prepare appliqué templates using patterns listed and provided on the insert for these tea towels: Tea Towel Flower and Stem; Bee Wing, Body and Stripe; Ladybug Head and Body; Leaf 2; Bird Body 1, Wings 1 and 2, Tail Feathers and Beak 1.

3. Trace appliqué shapes onto paper side of fusible web referring to list below for number to trace; cut out shapes. Apply shapes to wrong side of fabrics as listed below.

- Lime dot: 2 stems (1 reversed) and 2 leaf 2
- White tonal: 2 tea towel flowers (1 reversed) and 2 bee wings
- Yellow tonal: 1 bee body and 1 beak 1
- Red tonal: 1 ladybug body

- Black solid: 1 bee stripe and 1 ladybug head
- White with black crosshatch: 1 bird body 1
- Black with white dot: 1 each bird wing 1 and 2, and 1 tail feathers

4. Cut out appliqué shapes. Arrange stems and ladybug on chambray tea towel referring to Figure 1; arrange bird motif on lime green tea towel referring to Figure 2.

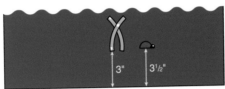

Figure 1

Figure 2

5. Arrange remaining appliqué shapes on towels; fuse in place.

6. Machine blanket-stitch around each appliqué shape using matching thread.

7. Following manufacturer's instructions, center interfacing strips and fuse to the wrong side of fabric strip as shown in Figure 3.

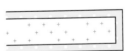

Figure 3

8. Press the long edges of the fabric over the edge of the interfacing to create a ½" hem as shown in Figure 4. Press a ½" hem in each short end.

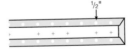

Figure 4

9. Pair yellow dot band with chambray towel and white with black dot band with lime green towel. Pin band on each towel 1⅜" from bottom edge of towel so top of band overlaps flower stems and touches bottom edge of ladybug. Stitch around each band near the edge using matching thread.

10. Machine-stitch bird legs twice using black thread. Sew black button to the bird for an eye and green flower-shape buttons to the white band.

11. Use two strands of white floss to make a French knot for ladybug's eye and two strands of black floss to make a French knot for bee's eye referring to patterns for positioning.

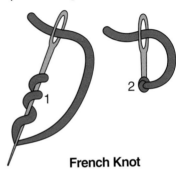

French Knot

12. Sew black-and-white buttons to the center of the flowers. ●

Busy Garden Tea Towels
Lime Green Towel
Placement Diagram
20" x 28"

Busy Garden Tea Towels
Chambray Towel
Placement Diagram
20" x 28"

Branching Out Table Runner

Brighten up your dining table with fresh colorful flowers. Add a touch of whimsical charm with yo-yo berries and a butterfly or two.

Skill Level
Confident Beginner

Specifications
Table Runner Size: 40" x 15"

Materials
- Small pieces medium green, lime, red, pink, lavender, aqua, dark blue, orange, yellow and light orange tonals
- Small piece black solid
- ¼ yard dark green tonal
- ⅓ yard black with white dot
- ⅝ yard white with black dot
- Backing to size
- Batting to size
- Thread
- Fusible web with paper release
- Compass or 2½"-diameter circle template
- Template material
- Basic sewing tools and supplies

Project Notes
Read all instructions before beginning this project.

Stitch right sides together using a ¼" seam allowance unless otherwise specified.

Refer to General Instructions on page 3 for specific construction and appliqué tips and techniques.

Materials and cutting lists assume 40" of usable fabric width.

Cutting

From dark blue tonal:
- Cut 9 (2½") squares. Using compass or circle template, cut a 2½"-diameter circle from each square to make 9 B circles.

From black with white dot:
- Cut 3 (2¼" by fabric width) binding strips.

From white with black dot:
- Cut 1 (15" x 40") A rectangle.

Completing the Table Runner
Refer to the Placement Diagram and project photo throughout for positioning of pieces.

1. Prepare appliqué templates using patterns listed and provided on the insert for this table runner: Vine 1; Tendrils 1, 2 and 3; Daisy Center; Daisy; Half Flower; Leaf 1; Flower Base; Butterfly Motif.

2. Trace appliqué shapes onto paper side of fusible web referring to list below for number to trace; cut out shapes. Apply shapes to wrong side of fabrics as listed below.

- Dark green tonal: 1 vine
- Medium green tonal: 1 each tendrils 1, 2 and 3; 2 flower bases
- Lime tonal: 6 leaves
- Red tonal and aqua tonal: 1 daisy each
- Pink tonal and lavender tonal: 1 half flower each
- Orange tonal: 1 butterfly wing, 1 small butterfly spot
- Yellow tonal: 2 daisy centers, 1 butterfly wing, 1 large butterfly spot
- Light orange tonal: 1 small butterfly spot, 1 large butterfly spot
- Black solid: 2 butterfly bodies

3. Cut out and arrange appliqué shapes on A rectangle beginning with the tendrils and then the vine and referring to the Vine 1 pattern and Figure 1 for positioning.

Figure 1

4. Arrange remaining appliqué shapes on A; fuse in place.

5. Machine blanket-stitch around each appliqué shape using matching thread.

6. Layer, quilt as desired and bind referring to General Instructions on page 3. Model is stitched around outside of each appliqué shape with matching threads. Tendrils are quilted in the blank areas and the leaves have double-stitched vein lines. Black thread is used to double-stitch the butterfly antennae.

7. Using B circles, make nine yo-yo's referring to Making Yo-Yo's below. Sew yo-yo's in groups of three along the vine. ●

Branching Out Table Runner
Placement Diagram 40" x 15"

Making Yo-Yo's

To make any size yo-yo:

1. Trace circle size desired using a template on wrong side of fabric.

2. Cut a length of thread to match fabric; double thread and knot ends together.

3. Working with wrong side of yo-yo circle facing you, turn under ¼" to wrong side and insert needle near the folded edge as shown in Figure A top image.

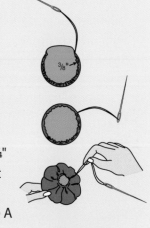

Figure A

4. Stitch a running stitch about ⅜" long around the edge of the circle, turning fabric edge under as you sew referring to Figure A center image. Stop stitching when you reach the beginning knot.

5. Pull thread to gather the circle as tightly as you can and move the hole to the center of the circle as seen in Figure A bottom image.

6. Insert needle between two gathers to the back of the yo-yo and make several small knots to secure; clip thread.

Here's a Tip

Select portions of this appliqué design to use on a smaller project, such as a place mat. A part of the vine with a flower and leaves going up the side of a 16" x 14" rectangle would work well and coordinate with the runner.

Microwave Bowl Cozies

These quick and easy microwave cozies are so useful when heating up food. Simply place the bowl inside the cozy and then into the microwave.

Skill Level
Confident Beginner

Specifications
Cozy Sizes: 5½" x 5½", 7" x 7", 8" x 8", 9½" x 9½", 11" x 11"

Materials
Materials listed make 5 cozies, 1 of each size.
- 1 cotton fat quarter each orange, lime, red, blue and green tonal
- ⅞ yard cotton black with white dot
- Cotton batting
- Cotton thread
- Basic sewing tools and supplies

Project Notes
It is important to use only 100 percent cotton fabric, batting and thread for these cozies because polyester may melt in a microwave and materials with metallic fibers will cause microwave to arc.

Read all instructions before beginning this project.

Stitch right sides together using a ¼" seam allowance unless otherwise specified.

Refer to General Instructions on page 3 for specific construction tips and techniques.

Materials and cutting lists assume 40" of usable fabric width.

Cutting

From orange tonal:
- Cut 1 (8") square.

From lime tonal:
- Cut 1 (9") square.

From red tonal:
- Cut 1 (10") square.

From blue tonal:
- Cut 1 (12") square.

From green tonal:
- Cut 1 (14") square.

From black with white dot:
- Cut 1 (14" by fabric width) strip.
  Subcut strip into 1 (14") square, 1 (12") square and 1 (10") square.
- Cut 1 (9" by fabric width) strip.
  Subcut strip into 1 (9") square and 1 (8") square.

From cotton batting:
- Cut 2 each 8" squares, 9" squares, 10" squares, 12" squares and 14" squares.

Completing the Bowl Cozies

1. Pin each fabric square to a same-size batting square with fabric right side up. With matching thread, stitch diagonally from corner to corner to quilt and secure the layers as shown in Figure 1.

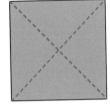

Figure 1

2. Fold one square in half with the fabric side in the center. Mark dart sewing lines as shown in Figure 2 referring to Dart Size Chart for specific measurements for each size square.

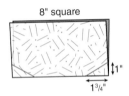
8" square
1"
1³/₄"

Figure 2

SQUARE SIZE	DART SIZE
8" x 8"	1" x 1³/₄"
9" x 9"	1" x 2"
10" x 10"	1" x 2¹/₄"
12" x 12"	1" x 2³/₄"
14" x 14"	1" x 3¹/₄"

Dart Size Chart

3. Stitch on the drawn dart lines, backstitching at both ends.

4. Repeat steps 2 and 3, folding the fabric the other direction and sewing darts to make a bowl-shaped unit as shown in Figure 3.

Figure 3

5. Repeat steps 2–4 with the second same-size batting-backed square to make two bowl-shaped units.

6. Trim excess batting from each dart by slipping your scissor tips between the batting and fabric, and then cutting the batting close to the dart seam as shown in Figure 4.

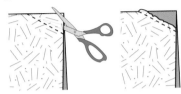

Figure 4

7. Nest same-size bowl-shaped units right sides together, matching corners and dart seams. Fold the darts in opposite directions to nest and pin in place. Sew a ¼" seam around all four sides, leaving a 3" opening for turning. Trim corners and batting close to the seam. Clip seam allowance on both sides of the dart as shown in Figure 5. ●

¼"

Figure 5

Here's a Tip

If you wish to make a cozy for a particular-size bowl, you can make one to fit. Measure the bowl down from the rim, across the bottom and up to the rim on the opposite side. Cut the fabric and batting squares to this measurement. Place the bowl in the center of a square and pinch the fabric together in the center of each side to determine the dart size needed.

Blooming Pot Holder Trio

Time to swap out the grimy pot holders hidden in the drawer for some colorful patchwork pieces that are as useful as they are decorative.

Skill Level

Confident Beginner

Specifications

Pot Holder Size: 8" x 8", excluding hanging loop

Materials

Materials listed make 1 of each style of pot holder.

- Scraps yellow and aqua dot, black solid and yellow tonal
- 1 fat quarter each pink, orange and red tonals
- ⅛ yard each lime dot and white with black dot
- ⅓ yard black with white dot
- 3 (8") squares cotton batting
- 3 (8") squares insulated batting
- 1 (³⁄₁₆") black button
- Thread
- Basic sewing tools and supplies

Project Notes

Read all instructions before beginning this project.

Stitch right sides together using a ¼" seam allowance unless otherwise specified.

Refer to General Instructions on page 3 for specific construction tips and techniques.

Materials and cutting lists assume 40" of usable fabric width.

Cutting

From yellow dot:
- Cut 4 (1½") C1 squares.

From aqua dot:
- Cut 4 (2½") B2 squares, 4 (1½") C2 squares, 2 (1" x 1¾") D rectangles and 1 (1¾" x 5") strip for hanging loop.

From black solid:
- Cut 1 (1" x 5½") E strip.

From yellow tonal:
- Cut 1 (1½" x 2") K rectangle.

From pink tonal:
- Cut 4 (4¼") A1 squares and 1 (8") backing square.

From orange tonal:
- Cut 4 (4" x 4¼") A2 rectangles and 1 (8") backing square.

From red tonal:

- Cut 1 (2") G square, 1 (2" x 5") I1 strip, 1 (2" x 3½") J1 rectangle, 2 (2¾") H1 squares and 1 (8") backing square.

From lime dot:

- Cut 1 (1¾" by fabric width) strip.
  Subcut strip into 12 (1¾") B1 squares and 1 (1¾" x 5") strip for hanging loop.

From white with black dot:

- Cut 2 (2¾") H2 squares, 1 (2" x 3½") J2 rectangle, 1 (2" x 5") I2 strip, 2 (2" x 8") L rectangles and 1 (1¾" x 5") strip for hanging loop.

From black with white dot:

- Cut 3 (2¼" by fabric width) binding strips.

Assembling the Flower Pot Holder

Refer to the Placement Diagram and project photo for positioning of pieces and stitching lines.

1. Draw a diagonal line on the wrong side of each B1 and C1 square.

2. Place a C1 square on one corner and B1 squares on remaining corners of A1 square referring to Figure 1.

Figure 1

3. Stitch on the drawn lines and trim seams to ¼" (Figure 2). Flip triangles and press.

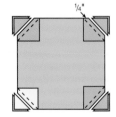

Figure 2

4. Repeat steps 2 and 3 to make four units.

5. Arrange units so yellow triangles are in the center. Sew units into rows; press. Sew rows together to complete the pot holder top; press.

6. Layer the pink tonal backing square, right side down; insulated batting, shiny side down; cotton batting square and the pieced top right side up and centered. Baste and quilt as desired. Model is stitched in the ditch of all seams and three lines were double-stitched in each petal.

7. Trim backing and batting to the same size as top if necessary.

8. To make the hanging loop, fold and press the lime dot hanging-loop strip lengthwise. Open and refold so the raw edges almost meet at the center crease (Figure 3); press.

Figure 3

9. Fold back in half again and topstitch the folded edges together (Figure 4).

Figure 4

10. Referring to Figure 5, pin the raw ends of the hanger on one corner of the pot holder back, about ¾" from the corner. Baste in place.

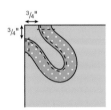

Figure 5

Inspiration

Any or all of these blocks would be appropriate for making a quilt. A quilt of flower, butterfly or bird blocks in different colors would make a wonderful baby quilt or throw. And all three blocks would combine nicely into one quilt as well.

11. Bind edges with the binding strip referring to General Instructions on page 3.

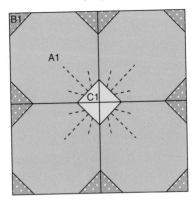

Flower Pot Holder
Placement Diagram 8" x 8"

Assembling the Butterfly Pot Holder

Refer to the Placement Diagram and project photo for positioning of pieces and stitching lines.

1. Draw a diagonal line on the wrong side of each B2 and C2 square.

2. Place a C2 square on one corner and a B2 square on the opposite corner of each A2 square referring to Figure 6.

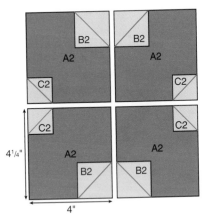

Figure 6

3. Stitch on the drawn lines and trim seams to ¼". Flip triangles and press.

4. Repeat steps 2 and 3 to make four corner units.

5. Sew D rectangles to short ends of E strip to make the center unit (Figure 7); press.

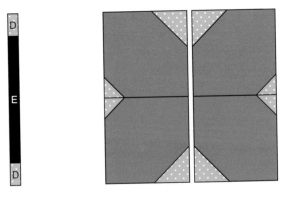

Figure 7   **Figure 8**

6. Join two corner units into vertical rows matching C2 seams together as shown in Figure 8; press.

7. Sew the center unit between the vertical rows to complete the pot holder top.

8. Follow steps 6–11 of Flower Pot Holder to layer, quilt, add hanging loop and bind the Butterfly Pot Holder using the orange tonal backing square and aqua dot hanging loop. Model is stitched in the ditch of all seams. Four large ovals are stitched in the orange tonal wings. Double-stitch antennae lines with black thread.

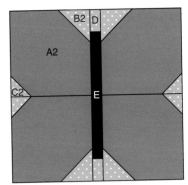

Butterfly Pot Holder
Placement Diagram 8" x 8"

Assembling the Bird Pot Holder

Refer to the Assembly Diagram and project photo for positioning of pieces and stitching lines.

1. Draw a diagonal line on the wrong side of each H2 square.

2. Referring to Figure 9, pair a marked H2 square with an H1 square, right sides together, and stitch ¼" away on both sides of drawn line. Cut on drawn line to make two H half-squares and press each open. Repeat to make two more H half-squares. Trim to 2" square, if needed.

Figure 9

3. Referring to Figure 10, arrange and sew three H half-squares, and 1 each G, I1 and J1 pieces into three rows; press. Sew the three rows together; press.

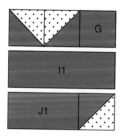

Figure 10

4. Sew an H half-square to one short end of the J2 rectangle as shown in Figure 11; press.

Figure 11

5. Position K rectangle at one short end of the I2 strip, right sides together. Referring to Figure 12, mark a dot ¾" down from the left corner and 1½" across; draw a line between the dots and stitch on the marked line.

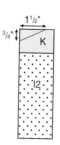

Figure 12

6. Flip the K piece up as shown in Figure 13; press. Trim the edges of K to match the corner of the I2 strip and trim the seam allowance to ¼".

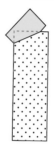

Figure 13

7. Arrange and sew units together to form the center unit; press. Sew L strips to top and bottom of the center unit to complete the pot holder top.

8. Follow steps 6–11 of Flower Pot Holder to layer, quilt, add hanging loop and bind the Bird Pot Holder using the red tonal backing square and the white with black dot hanging loop. Model is stitched in the ditch around the outline of the bird. A simple wing shape is quilted in the wing area. Double-stitch leg lines with black thread and sew on the black button for the bird's eye. ●

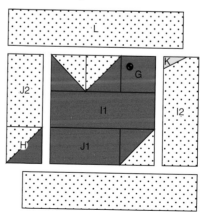

Bird Pot Holder
Assembly Diagram 8" x 8"

Birdhouse Pillow

This pillow would look perfect on a wicker chair or a porch swing.

Skill Level
Confident Beginner

Specifications
Pillow Size: 14" x 14", excluding ruffle

Materials
- Scrap black with white dot, light yellow tonal, yellow dot and black solid
- Fat quarter white tonal
- 1⅛ yards light blue tonal
- Cotton batting
- 14" x 14" pillow form
- 1 (³⁄₁₆") black button
- Polyester fiberfill
- Fusible web with paper release
- Template material
- Basic sewing tools and supplies

Project Notes
Read all instructions before beginning this project.

Stitch right sides together using a ¼" seam allowance unless otherwise specified.

Refer to General Instructions on page 3 for specific construction and appliqué tips and techniques.

Materials and cutting lists assume 40" of usable fabric width.

Cutting

From black with white dot:
- Cut 2 (6") D squares.

From white tonal:
- Cut 1 (7½") B square and 2 (4") E squares.

From light blue tonal:
- Cut 3 (7½" by fabric width) strips.
  Subcut strips into 2 (7½" x 30") ruffle strips, 2 (7½") C squares and 2 (4½" x 7½") A rectangles.
- Cut 1 (9½" by fabric width) strip.
  Subcut strip into 2 (9½" x 14½") rectangles for pillow backs.

From batting:
- Cut 1 (14½") square.

Assembling the Pillow
Refer to the Placement Diagram and project photo throughout for positioning of pieces.

1. Sew A rectangles to two opposite sides of the B square; press.

2. Draw a diagonal line on the wrong side of each D square and E square.

3. Place a D square on each C square, right sides together and matching one corner as shown in Figure 1.

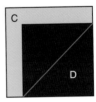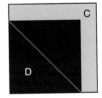

Figure 1

4. Stitch on the drawn line. Trim the seam to ¼" and flip the D pieces down and press (Figure 2).

Figure 2

5. Place the E squares on the D corners of the C-D units as shown in Figure 3.

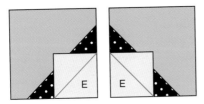

Figure 3

6. Stitch on the drawn line, trim the seam to ¼" and flip the E pieces down to press.

7. Sew the two C-D-E squares together, matching the D and E seams, to finish the top half of the birdhouse (Figure 4).

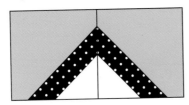

Figure 4

8. Sew the top and bottom halves together to complete the pieced pillow front; press.

9. Prepare templates using patterns listed and provided on the insert for this pillow: Birdhouse Hole 2, Beak 2, Bird Body 2 and Wing 3.

10. Trace three birdhouse hole appliqué shapes onto paper side of fusible web and cut out. Apply to wrong side of black solid.

11. Cut out the appliqué holes and arrange on pillow top, placing the lower hole 1½" up from the bottom edge with 1¼" spaces between each hole; fuse in place.

12. Machine blanket-stitch around each hole using matching thread.

13. Baste the pillow front to the batting square and quilt as desired. Model is stitched in the ditch of all the seams, around the holes and in vertical rows on the birdhouse.

14. Fold each ruffle strip in half lengthwise, right sides facing. Sew the short ends together (Figure 5). Clip the corners, turn right side out and press.

Figure 5

15. Make two rows of long machine gathering stitches ¼" and ⅛" away from the raw edges. Leave long threads at each end; do not backstitch at the ends.

16. Pull the bobbin threads at both sides until each ruffle measures 13¾" across (Figure 6). Knot threads and clip.

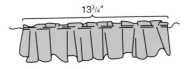

Figure 6

17. Pin a ruffle to each side of the pillow front, matching raw edges and leaving a margin of about ⅜" at each end (Figure 7). Sew the ruffles to the pillow using a ¼" seam allowance.

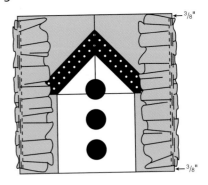

Figure 7

18. Press and sew a doubled ¼" hem on one 14½" end of each of the two pillow backs.

19. Place the pillow top right side up on work surface. With ruffles turned in toward the center, secure edges with pins to be sure ruffles don't get caught in the seam.

20. Pin a pillow back to each end of front, matching the raw edges and with the hemmed ends overlapping in the center. Sew all around with a ¼" seam allowance (Figure 8). Trim the corners and reach inside to remove the pins holding the ruffles. Turn right side out.

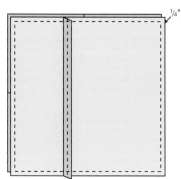

Figure 8

21. Referring to the Padded Appliqué instructions on page 4, use prepared templates to draw the following embellishment pieces on the wrong side of fabrics as listed below.

• Yellow tonal: 1 bird body 2
• Yellow dot: 2 wing 3 and 1 beak 2

22. Fold each marked fabric in half, right sides together, and pin wings and beak to scraps of batting. Do not pin the bird body to the batting at this time.

23. To complete the bird, follow steps 15–20 of Welcome Wreath on page 16.

24. Tack the bird to the front of the pillow, stitching in several places on the back of the bird. Insert pillow form into pillow to complete. ●

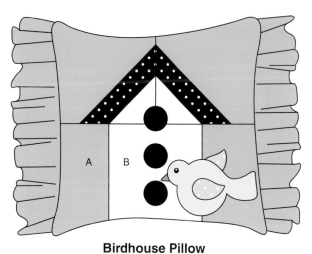

Birdhouse Pillow
Placement Diagram 14" x 14", excluding ruffle

In My Garden Sewing Accessories

Decorate your sewing space with a flowerpot pincushion, butterfly needle book and birdhouse chatelaine to keep necessities close at hand.

Project Notes

Read all instructions before beginning this project.

Stitch right sides together using a ¼" seam allowance unless otherwise specified.

Refer to General Instructions on page 3 for specific construction and appliqué tips and techniques.

Materials and cutting lists assume 40" of usable fabric width.

Flowerpot Pincushion

Skill Level
Confident Beginner

Specifications
Pincushion: 3" x 3½"

Materials

- Small piece each green tonal, and pink, red, orange and dark blue dot
- 2½" clay pot
- 3 flat-head pins
- 3 (¼") black-and-white buttons
- Craft glue
- Polyester fiberfill
- Thread
- Basic sewing tools and supplies

Cutting

From green tonal:
- Cut 1 (10") A circle.

From pink dot:
- Cut 1 (6") B circle.

From red, orange & dark blue dot:
- Cut 1 (3¼") C circle from each color.

Assembling the Pincushion

Refer to the Placement Diagram and project photo throughout for positioning of pieces.

1. Following the instructions for Making Yo-Yo's on page 32, sew the A circle into a large yo-yo, but do not turn under the edge as you gather stitch.

2. In the same manner, sew the B circle into a yo-yo without turning under the edge but before tightening the thread completely, stuff the yo-yo with fiberfill to form a firm ball.

Here's a Tip

Any (or all) of these accessories would make a lovely gift for a sewist or quilter. The Flowerpot Pincushion could be a fun favor for a luncheon; make one for every guest and write a name (or the menu) on a piece of paper and attach with one of the pins.

3. Apply a thin line of glue inside the top edge of the clay pot, about ¼" down. Carefully slip the green yo-yo inside the pot, leaving a ruffled edge about ½" above the rim of the pot.

4. Push the stuffed B yo-yo ball inside the green circle, applying small dots of glue if necessary to keep in place. It should fit very firmly inside the pot.

5. To make a five-petal flower, make a yo-yo with one of the C circles. After gathering and knotting the thread, bring the needle back up through the center hole. Take the thread over the edge of the yo-yo and back into the center and pull to form the start of one petal (Figure 1a). Take the thread over the edge again, on an adjacent side, and insert through center hole; pull to finish the first petal (Figure 1b). Continue around the yo-yo forming a total of five petals (Figure 1c). When flower is completed, knot and clip thread. Repeat with each of the C circles.

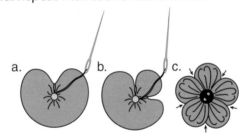

Figure 1

6. Sew a black-and-white button to the center of each flower to cover the center hole.

7. Glue the flat top of a pin to the center back of each flower to finish and insert into the pincushion.

In My Garden Sewing Accessories
Flowerpot Pincushion
Placement Diagram 3" x 3½"

Butterfly Needle Book

Skill Level
Confident Beginner

Specifications
Needle Book: 3½" x 7½", closed and excluding ties

Materials
- Scrap black with white dot
- ¼ yard each yellow and light orange tonals
- 18" of ⅝"-wide yellow grosgrain ribbon
- 20" of ¼"-wide black grosgrain ribbon
- 1 (⅝") black button
- Batting scraps
- Fusible web with paper release
- Thread
- Template material
- Basic sewing tools and supplies

Cutting

From yellow tonal:
- Prepare template using Butterfly Wings 1 pattern provided on the insert for needle book. Trace and cut 2 butterfly wings 1 pieces.

Assembling the Needle Book
1. Prepare templates using patterns listed and provided on the insert for this needle book: Butterfly Spot and Butterfly Wings 2.

2. Trace four butterfly spots onto paper side of fusible web and cut out. Draw a ¾" x 4" strip on the fusible web for the butterfly body and cut out. Apply cutout shapes to wrong side of fabrics as listed below.

- Light orange tonal: 4 butterfly spots and 1 butterfly wings 2
- Black with white dot: 1 butterfly body

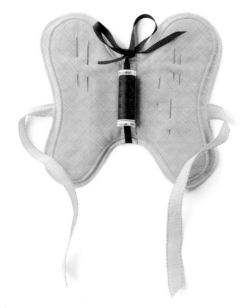

3. Referring to the Placement Diagram and project photo, position one spot on each section of one butterfly wings 1 piece for front; place the body strip in the center. Fuse in place.

4. Machine blanket-stitch around each appliqué shape using matching thread.

5. Cut the yellow ribbon in half and place an end of each length of yellow ribbon on opposite sides of the butterfly wings 1 front where indicated on pattern. The raw edges of the ribbon should be even with the raw edges of the fabric. Baste in place.

6. Cut the black ribbon into two lengths: 8" and 12". Place the lengths of black ribbon at the center of the butterfly with the 8" length at the top and the 12" length at the bottom. Baste in place.

7. Fold up all the ribbon lengths and hold with a pin so they do not get caught in the stitching except where they are attached.

8. Using the remaining butterfly wings 1 piece for backing, place the backing over the top of the front piece, right sides facing and matching edges. Pin both layers to a piece of batting. Sew all around with a ¼" seam. Clip the curves and cut a slash down the center of the backing only. Turn right side out through the slash; unpin the ribbons and pull them free. Whipstitch the slash edges together and press the butterfly from front side so the edges are smooth and flat. Topstitch the wings ⅛" from the edge.

9. Quilt as desired. Model is stitched around the spot appliqués.

10. Use prepared template to trace the butterfly wings 2 shape on the wrong side of the light orange tonal. Fold the fabric in half, right sides facing, and pin to a doubled stack of batting. Sew all around on the traced lines. Cut out ⅛" from the seam and clip the curves. Cut a slash down the center through one layer of fabric only. Turn right side out through the slash. Whipstitch slash edges together and press. Topstitch all around ⅛" from the edge.

11. Center the orange butterfly wings on the backing piece of the appliquéd butterfly, with the slashed sides facing, and pin. Turn butterfly over and stitch on both sides of the appliquéd black body strip to attach.

12. Sew the black button to the top of the black strip for butterfly's head.

13. To finish, thread the longer black ribbon through the center of a small spool of thread. Bring the ribbon to the top and tie the two ends of black ribbons in a bow.

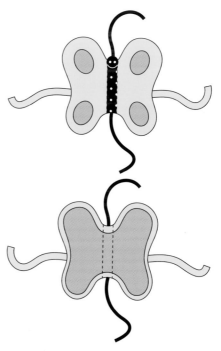

In My Garden Sewing Accessories
Butterfly Needle Book
Placement Diagram 3½" x 7½",
closed and excluding ties

Birdhouse Chatelaine

Skill Level
Confident Beginner

Specifications
Chatelaine: 4" x 5¾", excluding strap

Materials
- Scraps each aqua tonal and black solid
- ⅛ yard each white with black dot and aqua with white dot
- Batting scraps
- Fusible web with paper release
- Thread
- Template material
- Basic sewing tools and supplies

Cutting

From aqua tonal:
- Cut 4 (1¼" x 4½") A strips.

From white with black dot:
- Prepare templates using pattern, cut 2 birdhouses and 2 birdhouse linings.

From aqua with white dot:
- Cut 1 (1¼" x 36") strip for strap.

Assembling the Chatelaine

1. Pin one A strip to the top edge of a birdhouse, right sides facing. Strip is longer than needed so let it overlap on both ends. Sew with a ¼" seam (Figure 2a). Flip the strip over and press; trim the ends to match the top of the birdhouse piece (Figure 2b). Sew an A strip to the opposite edge of the birdhouse. Flip, press, and trim (Figure 2c).

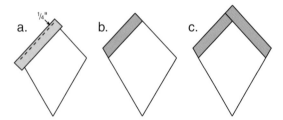

Figure 2

2. Repeat step 1 with the second birdhouse and remaining A strips.

3. Prepare a template for the birdhouse hole 1 using pattern provided on the insert and trace onto the paper side of fusible web; cut out. Apply to the wrong side of the black solid.

4. Cut out hole and center on one of the birdhouse pieces; fuse in place. This will be the front birdhouse piece.

5. Machine blanket-stitch the edges of hole using black thread.

6. Fold the strap strip in half lengthwise, wrong sides together, and press. Open the strip and fold each long raw edge to the inside so edges almost meet at the center fold line (Figure 3a); press. Refold the strip again on the first fold line. Topstitch down both long edges to finish strap (Figure 3b).

Figure 3

7. Pin the strap ends to the right side of the birdhouse back, ¾" from the outer corners (Figure 4). Baste in place.

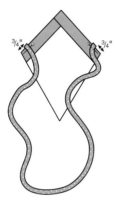

Figure 4

8. Pin a lining piece over the back, right sides together. Move the strap to one side so it can hang out of the space left for an opening. Stitch all around, leaving a 2" opening on one side (Figure 5). Trim the corners and turn right side out, pulling the strap free. Fold in the seam allowance and slip-stitch closed.

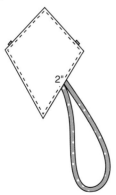

Figure 5

9. Pin the remaining lining piece to the birdhouse front, right sides together, and sew all around, leaving a 2" opening on one side. Trim the corners and turn right side out. Fold in the seam allowance and slip-stitch closed.

10. Quilt the front and back if desired. Model is stitched in the ditch between the roof and house and around the birdhouse hole appliqué.

11. Pin the birdhouse front and back together, lining sides facing; hand-sew pieces together with a short slip stitch, stitching between the front and back lining layers on the two lower sides. ●

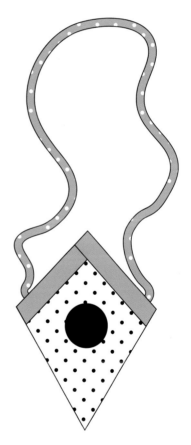

In My Garden Sewing Accessories
Birdhouse Chatelaine
Placement Diagram 4" x 5¾",
excluding strap

Bursting Into Bloom Bed Runner

This runner will perk up any bed with its bright and beautiful dimensional flowers.

Skill Level
Confident Beginner

Specifications
Bed Runner Size: 80" x 14", excluding extending leaves

Materials
- ¼ yard dark yellow tonal
- ⅓ yard black with white dot
- ⅜ yard each aqua , dark blue and light yellow tonals
- ½ yard each pink and orange tonals
- ⅝ yard red tonal
- ¾ yard green tonal
- 2½ yards white with black cross hatch
- Cotton batting
- Thread
- Template material
- Fusible web with paper release
- Basic sewing tools and supplies

Project Notes
Read all instructions before beginning this project.

Stitch right sides together using a ¼" seam allowance unless otherwise specified.

Refer to General Instructions on page 3 for specific construction and appliqué tips and techniques.

Materials and cutting lists assume 40" of usable fabric width.

Cutting

From white with black crosshatch:
- Cut 2 (14½" x 80½") A rectangles

From cotton batting:
- Cut 1 (14½" x 80½") rectangle, 6 (7") squares, 4 (10") squares, 2 (13") squares, 1 (15") square and 10 (5" x 9") rectangles.

Assembling the Bed Runner
Refer to the Padded Appliqué instructions on page 4 to make flowers and leaves. Refer to the Placement Diagram and project photo throughout for positioning of pieces.

1. Layer 14½" x 80½" batting rectangle, one A rectangle right side up and second A rectangle right side down. Stitch through all layers around edges, leaving a 5" opening on one side. Trim batting close to the seam; trim corners and turn right side out. Fold in opening seam allowance and slip-stitch closed. Press the edges smooth and flat.

2. Quilt as desired. Model is stitched with a large grid, about 3½" apart, over the runner and topstitched ¼" from the edge.

3. Prepare templates using Flowers & Flower Center Circles patterns listed and provided on the insert for this bed runner: 1¾", 2¼", 3", 3½", 4", 5", 6", 9", 12" and 14" Circles and Leaf 3.

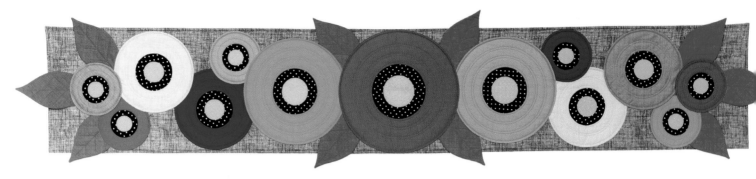

4. Use the 6", 9", 12" and 14" circle templates and the batting squares (pair circles with squares that are 1" larger) to make flowers from fabrics listed below.

- 6" flowers: 1 each aqua tonal, orange tonal, blue tonal and pink tonal, and 2 red tonal
- 9" flowers: 1 each aqua tonal, blue tonal and 2 light yellow tonal
- 12" flowers: 1 each orange tonal and pink tonal
- 14" flowers: 1 red

5. To make flower centers, trace appliqué circles onto paper side of fusible web referring to list below for number to trace; cut out. Apply circles to wrong side of fabrics as listed below.

- Black with white dot: 6 (3") circles, 4 (4") circles, 2 (5") circles and 1 (6") circle
- Dark yellow tonal: 6 (1¾") circles, 4 (2¼") circles, 2 (3") circles and 1 (3½") circle

6. Cut out and arrange dark yellow tonal circles on black with white dot circles, pairing smallest circles of each fabric progressively up to the largest. Again, pairing sizes, position flower centers onto a flower with the smallest centers on the 6" flowers and the largest center on the 14" flower; fuse in place.

7. Machine blanket-stitch around each black and yellow center circle using matching thread.

8. Quilt each flower as desired. Model is quilted in concentric circles using matching threads.

9. Make 10 padded leaves with green tonal fabric using prepared template and 5" x 9" batting rectangles. Referring to pattern, double-stitch vein lines in each leaf using green thread.

10. Arrange the 13 flowers and 10 leaves on the runner. The large red flower is in the center with six flowers on each side in the same size arrangement but with different colors. ***Note:*** *The flowers overlap each other and the raw edges of the leaves are all tucked securely under flowers.* When satisfied with the arrangement, pin in place.

11. Starting with one of the flowers on the bottom layer, remove pins from the overlapped edges and fold the top flowers back enough so that you can stitch the flower to the quilted runner. Use a walking or even-feed foot and sew ¼" from the edge of the flowers, using matching thread.

12. Continue stitching down the flowers from the bottom layer to the ones on top layer. Catch the base of the leaves in the stitches and keep the tips of leaves free. ●

Here's a Tip

The individual flowers can be used to embellish other quilted projects. Try a few small ones on pillows or a table runner and make the large ones to use as place mats.

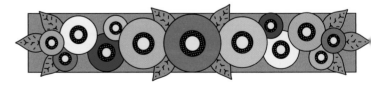

Bursting Into Bloom Bed Runner
Placement Diagram 80" x 14",
excluding extending leaves

Bloom Row Quilt

This colorful row quilt is a sampler of the many projects in this book, plus a few new blocks for fun. Now you can make a complete look for any room in your home.

Skill Level
Confident Beginner

Specifications
Quilt Size: 54½" x 64½"
Block Sizes: 8" x 8" finished
Number of Blocks: 14

Materials
- Fat quarter each black solid; dark blue, aqua, light orange, orange, green, dark green, lavender, pink, dark pink, lime and red tonals; and pink, yellow and lime dots
- ½ yard black with white dot
- ⅔ yard aqua dot
- 1 yard white tonal
- 1⅝ yards each light blue, light and dark yellow tonals, and white with black dot
- Backing to size
- Batting to size
- 5 (7") batting squares
- 3 yards fusible web with paper release
- 7 (⅝") white buttons
- 7 (³⁄₁₆") black buttons
- Thread
- Template material
- Basic sewing tools and supplies

Project Notes
Read all instructions before beginning this project.

Stitch right sides together using a ¼" seam allowance unless otherwise specified.

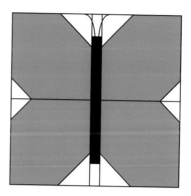

Butterfly
8" x 8" Finished Block
Make 7

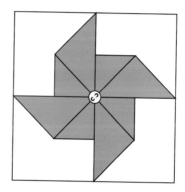

Pinwheel
8" x 8" Finished Block
Make 7

Refer to General Instructions on page 3 for specific construction and appliqué tips and techniques.

Materials and cutting lists assume 40" of usable fabric width.

Refer to the Placement Diagram and project photo throughout for positioning of pieces.

Cutting

From black solid:
• Cut 7 (1¼" x 5½") E2 strips

From dark blue tonal:
• Cut 15 (2½") squares. Using compass or circle template, cut a 2½"-diameter circle from each square to make 15 D circles.

From aqua tonal:
• Cut 4 (1¾" x 8½") C strips.

From pink, yellow & lime dots, & orange, green & lavender tonals:
• Cut 4 each color (4⅛" x 4½") A2 rectangles to cut 24 A2 rectangles.

From orange, lavender, aqua, pink & dark blue tonals:
• Cut 1 each color (7" x 14") E rectangle for a total of 5 E rectangles.

From red, aqua, orange, dark blue, pink, medium green & dark yellow tonals:
• Cut 4 each color (4½") F squares for a total of 28 F squares.

From white tonal:
• Cut 2 (2¾" by fabric width) strips.
    Subcut strips into 28 (2¾") B2 squares.
• Cut 2 (1¾" by fabric width) strips.
    Subcut strips into 28 (1¾") C2 squares. Trim remainder of strip to 1¼" wide and subcut strip into 14 (1¼" x 2") D2 rectangles.
• Cut 4 (4½" by fabric width) strips.
    Subcut strips into 28 (4½") G squares.

From aqua dot:
• Cut 2 (8½" by fabric width) strips.
    Subcut strips into 3 (8½" x 9½") A rectangles and 2 (8½" x 12½") B rectangles.
    Trim remainder of strips and subcut 4 (4⅛" x 4½") A2 rectangles.

From black with white dot:
• Cut 6 (2¼" by fabric width) binding strips.

From light & dark yellow tonals:
• Cut 1 each color (54½" by fabric width) strip. Subcut 1 each color (8½" x 54½") background strip.

From white with black dot & light blue tonal:
• Cut 1 each color (54½" by fabric width) strip. Subcut 1 each color (12½" x 54½") background strip.

Completing the Bloom Row

1. Prepare appliqué templates using patterns listed and provided on the insert for this row: Daisy and Daisy Center; Butterfly Body, Wing, Small Spot and Large Spot; Letters B, L and M; Tulip Petal 2; Vine 2; Leaf 4 and Leaf 5.

2. Trace appliqué shapes onto paper side of fusible web referring to list below for number to trace; cut out. Apply shapes to wrong side of fabrics as listed below.

• White tonal: 2 daisies (reverse 1)
• Pink tonal: 6 tulip petals 2
• Dark pink tonal: 6 tulip petals 2
• Lime tonal: 2 vine 2 (reverse 1); 4 leaf 4 (reverse 2); 8 leaf 5 (reverse 4)
• Dark yellow tonal: 2 daisy centers; 1 butterfly large spot
• Aqua dot: 1 each letters B, L and M
• Orange tonal: 1 butterfly wing
• Light orange: 1 butterfly small spot
• Black solid: 1 butterfly body

3. Cut out appliqué shapes and arrange on light yellow tonal background strip. Referring to Figure 1, start with the vines, placing the end of each vine 3¼" in from the side and 3¼" up from the bottom.

Figure 1

4. Add remaining appliqué shapes placing the "B" over the right end of the left vine and the "M" over the left end of the right vine. Add the "L" and two daisies to complete the word. The tulips are formed with two pink and one dark pink petals and two dark pink combined with one pink to make each flower to go on the end of the stems. Place a leaf on the outer end of each vine and distribute the remaining leaves along the vine and beside one daisy as shown. Add the butterfly to the side of the other daisy to complete the arrangement; fuse in place.

5. Machine blanket-stitch around each appliqué shape using matching thread. Double-stitch the butterfly antennae with black thread.

Completing the Sunshine & Sprinkles Row

1. Prepare appliqué templates using patterns listed and provided on the insert for this row: Large Half Sun, Long Sun Ray, Short Sun Ray, Umbrella, Umbrella Handle and Boot.

2. Trace appliqué shapes onto paper side of fusible web referring to list below for number to trace; cut out. Apply shapes to wrong side of fabrics as listed below.

- Light yellow tonal: 2 large half suns
- Orange tonal: 6 long sun rays
- Dark yellow tonal: 8 short sun rays
- White with black dots: 3 umbrellas
- Black solid: 3 umbrella handles
- Red tonal: 6 boots (reverse 3)

3. Cut out appliqué shapes and arrange on A and B rectangles. Center a large half sun at the 12½" bottom edge of each B rectangle. Space the short and long rays around the sun, alternating the colors as shown, with the sun overlapping the lower ends. With the 9½" edge at the top and bottom, place an umbrella and handle, and a pair of boots on each A rectangle, making sure edges of shapes are not in seam allowance.

4. Machine blanket-stitch around each appliqué shape using matching thread. Stitch black contour lines on the umbrellas as shown on pattern.

5. Arrange the five blocks, starting and ending with an umbrella block and alternating with the sun blocks. Place a C sashing strip between the blocks.

6. Sew the blocks and sashing strips together to finish the row; press.

Completing the Flowerpot Row

1. Prepare appliqué templates using patterns listed and provided on the insert for this row: Flowerpot; Vine 1; Tendrils 1 and 2; Half Flower and Flower Base; Daisy and Daisy Center; Butterfly Body, Wing, Small Spot and Large Spot; and Leaf 1.

2. Trace appliqué shapes onto paper side of fusible web referring to list below for number to trace; cut out. Apply shapes to wrong side of fabrics as listed below.

- Red tonal: 1 flowerpot
- Dark green tonal: 2 vine 1 (reverse 1)
- Green tonal: 2 tendril 2 (reverse 1); 2 tendril 1 (reverse 1); 2 flower bases
- Lime tonal: 11 leaf 1
- Orange tonal: 2 daisies (reverse 1); 3 butterfly small spots
- Aqua tonal: 2 daisies (reverse 1)
- Dark yellow tonal: 4 daisy centers; 3 butterfly wings (reverse 1)
- Lavender tonal: 2 half flowers
- Light orange: 3 butterfly large spots
- Black solid: 3 butterfly bodies (reverse 1)

3. Cut out appliqué shapes and arrange on white with black dot background strip. Referring to Figure 2, start with flowerpot in the center, placing it 1½" up from the bottom edge. Add the two vines going in opposite directions with the starting end tucked under the top edge of the pot. The vines should end about 7½" from the side edges of the background strip and 2½" up from the bottom edge.

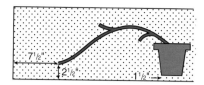

Figure 2

4. Arrange the tendrils, flowers and leaves along the vines, tucking the ends of the tendrils under the vines. Place the flower base pieces over the bottom of half flowers and the end of the vine stems. Place a daisy center on each daisy. Add the butterflies as shown. When satisfied with the arrangement, fuse in place.

5. Machine blanket-stitch around each appliqué shape using matching threads. Double-stitch the butterfly antennae with black thread.

6. To make the yo-yo berries, follow Making Yo-Yo's on page 32 to make 15 yo-yo's from the D circles. Set aside to add to the row after the quilting is complete.

Completing the Butterfly Row

1. Draw a diagonal line on the wrong side of each B2 and C2 square.

2. Place a C2 square on one corner and a B2 square on opposite corners of an A2 rectangle referring to Figure 3. Repeat on corners of three remaining same-color A2 rectangles.

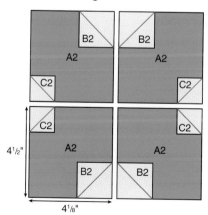

Figure 3

3. Stitch on the drawn lines and trim seams to ¼". Flip B and C pieces and press to complete four corner units.

4. Sew two D2 pieces to short ends of one E strip (Figure 4) to complete a center unit; press.

Figure 4

5. Join two corner units to make a vertical row matching C2 piece seams together (Figure 5); press. Repeat with two remaining corner units.

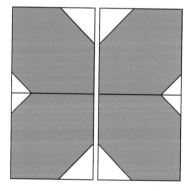

Figure 5

6. Referring to the block drawing, position center unit between two vertical rows and sew together to complete one Butterfly block.

7. Repeat steps 2–6 with the remaining A2–E2 pieces to make a total of seven Butterfly blocks.

8. Machine double-stitch antennae lines to each Butterfly block with black thread.

9. Arrange the seven blocks into a horizontal row referring to the Placement Diagram, alternating the direction of the butterflies as shown. Sew the blocks together.

Completing the Bird & Birdhouse Row

1. Prepare appliqué templates using patterns listed and provided on the insert for this row: Cloud, Birdhouse 2, Birdhouse Hole 3 and Roof; Bird Body 1, Wings 1 and 2, Tail Feathers and Singing Bird Beak.

2. Trace appliqué shapes onto paper side of fusible web referring to list below for number to trace; cut out shapes. Apply shapes to wrong side of fabrics as listed below.

- White tonal: 2 clouds (reverse 1)
- White with black dot: 3 birdhouses 2
- Black with white dot: 3 roofs
- Black solid: 3 birdhouse holes 3
- Aqua tonal: 1 bird body 1
- Aqua dot: 1 each wing 1, wing 2 and tail feathers
- Light yellow tonal: 1 bird body 1 (reverse pattern)
- Yellow dot: 4 singing bird beaks; 1 each wing 1, wing 2 and tail feathers
- Pink tonal: 1 bird body 1 (reverse pattern)
- Pink dot: 1 each wing 1, wing 2 and tail feathers
- Lime tonal: 1 bird body 1 (reverse pattern)
- Lime dot: 1 each wing 1, wing 2 and tail feathers

3. Cut out appliqué shapes and arrange on light blue background strip. Referring to Figure 6 for positioning, start with the birdhouses, one centered on the bottom edge of strip and the other two 10¼" away from top edge of the center one.

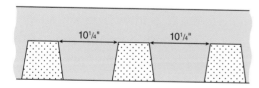

10¼"   10¼"

Figure 6

4. Arrange the remaining appliqué shapes, placing a roof on each birdhouse, overlapping the top edge ¼", and centering a hole appliqué 1" down from the roof edge. Add a bird with beak and color-matched wings and tail feather on each end and between the birdhouses. Position a cloud between the birdhouses, 1½" down from the top edge. When satisfied with the arrangement, fuse in place.

5. Machine blanket-stitch around the appliqué shapes using matching threads.

6. Draw stick legs for each bird and double-stitch with black thread.

Completing the Big Bloom Row

1. Prepare templates using patterns listed and provided on the insert for this row: 1¾" and 3" Centers, 6" Flower and Leaf 6.

2. Trace the circle flower shape on the wrong side of each E rectangle at one end; fold the fabric in half, right sides facing and traced shape on top; pin to a 7" square of batting.

3. Sew around on the marked circle. Cut out ⅛" from the seam using pinking shears. If using regular shears, clip the curves generously. Cut a slash in the center through one layer of fabric only and turn each flower right side out through the slash. Press the edges smooth and flat. Set aside.

4. Trace appliqué shapes onto paper side of fusible web referring to list below for number to trace; cut out. Apply shapes to wrong side of fabrics as listed below.

- Aqua, pink, yellow and lime dots, and white with black dot: 1 each 3" center
- Yellow tonal: 5 (1¾") centers
- Orange, lavender, aqua, pink and dark blue tonals: 1 each 6" flower
- Lime dot: 8 leaf 6

5. Cut out appliqué shapes and center a 3" center on each of the circle flower fronts (the side that is not slashed); fuse in place. Center a 1¾" center on the dot centers of each flower and fuse in place.

6. Machine blanket-stitch the edges of the appliqué shapes on each flower using matching threads.

7. Quilt a circle 1" from the outer edge of each circle flower using matching threads.

8. Arrange the five flowers and eight leaves across the dark yellow background strip, placing the center aqua flower 1¾" up from the bottom. The orange and dark blue flowers are ¾" up from the bottom and 1½" in from the side edges. The lavender and pink flowers are centered between the other flowers, 1¾" up from the bottom. Pin them in place but do not stitch down at this point.

9. Arrange the leaf appliqués as shown, lifting the edge of the flowers to tuck the leaf ends under. Fuse the leaves in place.

10. Machine blanket-stitch around the leaves using matching thread.

11. Attach the flowers by sewing ¼" from the edge using matching threads.

Completing the Dimensional Pinwheel Row

1. Fold all F squares in half diagonally, right sides out, as shown in Figure 7; press.

Figure 7

2. Place a folded F triangle on a G square, lining up the raw edges on two adjacent sides. Baste across one side, ³⁄₁₆" from the edge (Figure 8).

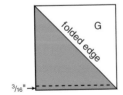

Figure 8

3. Fold the tip of the triangle that is not secured with basting stitches down to the bottom corner, making a little pocket. Baste along the raw edge to hold (Figure 9).

Figure 9

4. Repeat steps 2 and 3 using all the folded F triangles and G squares to make 28 F-G units.

5. Arrange four same-color F-G units into two rows of two units each in a pinwheel shape (Figure 10). Sew the two units together in each row; press seams open.

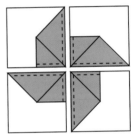

Figure 10

6. Sew the two rows together; press seams open.

7. Repeat steps 5 and 6 to make a total of seven Pinwheel blocks.

8. Referring to the Placement Diagram, arrange the Pinwheel blocks in a horizontal row and sew the blocks together; press the seams open.

Completing the Quilt

1. Referring to the Placement Diagram and project photo, arrange the seven rows as shown and sew the rows together; press.

2. Follow the instructions for Finishing Your Quilt in General Instructions on page 3 to quilt and bind the quilt.

3. Sew a black button to the top of each umbrella in the Sunshine & Sprinkles row.

4. Arrange the 15 blue yo-yo berries along the vine on the Flowerpot row and hand-appliqué the edges in place.

5. Sew a black button to the head of each bird for an eye in the Bird & Birdhouse row.

6. Sew a white button to the center of each pinwheel on the Dimensional Pinwheel row. ●

Here's a Tip

Many of these blocks and rows could be used in other ways. Make mug rugs from the Sunshine & Sprinkles blocks or combine a daisy and a butterfly from the Flowerpot row to make a pretty mug rug. Make any of the long appliquéd rows into interesting runners for the table or a narrow buffet. The Butterfly blocks or the dimensional Pinwheel blocks would make a colorful quilt. Use your imagination and these patterns to develop designs that work in your home.

Bloom Row Quilt
Placement Diagram 54¹/₂" x 64¹/₂"

Supplies

We would like to thank the following manufacturers who provided materials to make sample projects for this book.

Pin Dot, Dot, Sketch and Hatch Basic fabrics from Timeless Treasures.

Dream Cotton Select batting from Quilters Dream Batting.

Fusible web and fusible interfacing from Bosal Foam.

Tea towels from Dunroven House.

In addition, the author would like to thank professional longarm quilter Jean McDaniel for her work on the Bloom Row Quilt.

Annie's®   *Birds, Butterflies & Blooms* is published by Annie's, 306 East Parr Road, Berne, IN 46711. Printed in USA. Copyright © 2015, 2016 Annie's.

RETAIL STORES: If you would like to carry this publication or any other Annie's publications, visit AnniesWSL.com.

Every effort has been made to ensure that the instructions in this publication are complete and accurate. We cannot, however, take responsibility for human error, typographical mistakes or variations in individual work. Please visit AnniesCustomerService.com to check for pattern updates.

ISBN: 978-1-59012-353-9

2 3 4 5 6 7 8 9